The Struggle

The Struggle

Compiled and Edited by:
Austin Mardon Rebecca Ryan
Brey Dawson Jessica Jutras

Design and Typset by:
Paige Prins

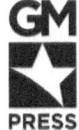

Copyright © 2022 by Austin Mardon
All rights reserved.
This book or any portion thereof may not be reproduced or used in any manner whatsoever without the express written permission of the publisher except for the use of brief quotations in a book review or scholarly journal.
First Printing: 2022

Cover Design by Paige Prins
Typeset by Paige Prins

ISBN: 978-1-77369-874-8
eBook ISBN: 978-1-77369-875-5

Golden Meteorite Press
103 11919 82 St NW
Edmonton, AB T5B 2W3
www.goldenmeteoritepress.com

Dedication

This book is dedicated to those that grind the 9-5 everyday, just to come home and see that their dog threw up on the carpet. Life is messy and unexpected, full of bills and broken dreams. But through the rage and chaos of our lives, we gain experience and uncover truths about ourselves and those that surround us. This anthology simply could not exist without the help of the creatives that filled these pages with their personal experiences and imaginative story-telling.

Thank you to each writer who trusted us enough to contribute a piece of themselves into their work for us to share with our readers.

Thank you to the Antarctic Institute of Canada for making this project possible. We, as writers, are beyond grateful and honoured to have been a part of this.

Contents

Smile Smile Smile	*Madeline Medensky*	2
Point-Loss	*Madeline Medensky*	3
Adrift	*Ashley Witiw*	4
Void	*Ashley Witiw*	5
One on One	*Kyra Droog*	6
Untouched	*Cora Dallyn*	8
Untitled	*Travis O'Neil*	9
Through the Veil	*Brandon Tilt*	10
The Protagonist	*Electus*	12
Life's Poem	*Electus*	13
Wildflower	*Samantha Skeich*	14
The Drive	Samantha Skeich	15
Coping	*Josh Harnack*	16
The Sabotage Loop	*Kian Isaac*	17
For Nelson	*Kristopher Hinz*	18
Bitter	*Stefani Litwin*	20
Still Bitter	*Stefani Litwin*	21
Jim Carrey	*Brey*	22
The Unspoken Poet	*Brandon Tilt*	24
Rotten too	*Sabryn Jones*	26
Folktales for the Dead	*Sabryn Jones*	27
Post-Anxiety	*Electus*	28
Tomorrow	*Electus*	29

Bromeliad	*Ashley Witiw*	30
Hollow	*Ashley Witiw*	31
Slipping	*Samantha Skeich*	32
Enthralled	*Rebecca Ryan*	33
Love, I Loved You	*Madeline Medensky*	34
Giants, I'm Just a Girl	*Madeline Medensky*	35
Inferno	*Peter Anto Johnson*	36
Morning rage	*John Christy Johnson*	37
I'm the girl	*Stefani Litwin*	38
I don't wanna love you anymore	*Stefani Litwin*	39
Ever Since	*Daniel Klassen*	40
Head Tilt Chin Lift	*Daniel Klassen*	41
Sirens	*Brandon Tilt*	42
Untitled	*Mark O'Reilly*	44
Untitled	*JJ*	45
I don't know how long it's been	*Rebecca Ryan*	46
Unknown	*Isabella Anderson*	47
Peter Paranoia	*Daniel Klassen*	48
Overdraft	*Daniel Klassen*	49
Edgelord	*Brey*	50
Untitled	*Tianna*	51
Cavalier	*Riley Witiw*	52

Smile Smile Smile
A poem by Madeline Medensky

Claire stopped driving 'cause gas prices
peaked and what she can't carry
so I pick her up in my truck that's rusting
between the gas plates, window panes
Claire's 53
she slides in, pink and full says,
"girl, start treating your wrinkles"
I'm 25
what do you, you mean we were
going downtown past the tent city
mini-country, smoked out with its dirt-dust,
shopping carts puttered with tarp and ramtops,
Claire casts a glare and says "I'm close to there"
not yet, not really, choked with a worry she won't hold back
but laugh at these streets slide away in sharp, stagnant sun
plunging into bills, restaurants, charred grass
yellowed and parched, removed away from
its greener, greater bide
I want to say what i think but can't
I wonder now how to make this life
and make it and make it and make it again
from my parents' house, from the way right, from the
politician's politic fallacies, from the Arts major salary,
from the price-picked day prick,
from the malady of meaning nice but coming across mean,
from the online screen and blank sheet, from the man
on the Bumble plan holding a fish or three, from
the hookup him, from the online mummer, from the
2.99 (!!) cucumbers, from the breath and the breath
and the breathing and the Claire smiles, wind-wide
no scathing sort of thought can hide her cheek lines.

Point-Loss
A poem by Madeline Medensky

Is there a point here?
Is there a point to its loss?
the black night is star-full
like a jar of antibiotics
and the septic cleanse cleans the roads right
life thrums with its second-sound
dogs lie awake by tv screens, daffodils close
(the whole world smells like them), the rain
parts its plan and doesn't come again, a man
scrounges around around in a sandbox dappled
by a moon (purple and plump), I'm replaying
replaying today here – an office, an apartment clogged
up, hanging up (her hanging up on me), screaming, losing
its cool, its plenty, its fistful of fuck you's, its storm, its bash bash
bashing back to me, me throwing up tears,
hurling away my complacency, knowing
I didn't do enough or I did, I did too much, knowing billionaires
exist, knowing politics are corrupt, knowing my mom loves me,
when it's hard (what I walk away from), knowing life
is buoyant but why do I feel I sink, what pulls pulls up,
what takes words back (or doesn't), what matters when I'm mute,
when I have nothing to prove but life is just starting, starting here,
in a washed, walked town, in the purge of young (little, I'm talking little girl),
in the curved curiosity, in the passion-starved day job… I wonder I wonder,
the words crawl away from, and sound is non-language—trees stiffed
by a breeze pulled over itself, bugs, crickets, cradle-hugs, candles somewhere,
salty lumps of lard cooling, or wedding bands on tabletops,
sleep, ears turned off, it's quiet here and there is nothing.

Adrift
A Poem by Ashley Witiw

Sorrow ripples across the glass sea of my heart,
I hold a spinning compass, a torn map.
I am adrift,
enveloped in the grey mists of uncertainty.

Tears write apologies on the paper remnants
of a life--half followed, half dreamed,
but never to be,
As silence descends over a stilled sea.

Void
A Poem by Ashley Witiw

I've seen into your deepest depths
Lured inside and abandoned to discover
The cruel, empty cold of your innermost sanctum,
The yawning void of a soul who will never be fulfilled,
Where you gnash and crush those you've lured
With the hollow glimmer of your sharpened, silver tongue

One on One
A Poem by Kyra Droog

The needle drops;
deafening silence.
You wait, breath tucked into your chest like a child tucked into her sheets,
protected from the evil of the dark.
Will the music come?
When?
Inhale
Exhale
There.
The static hisses.
Much like the rain, like fingers tapping on your window in the night.
Like a song, but more subdued, lyrical.
Welcoming you home.
You smile.
Inhale
Exhale
Finally.
The piano begins.
Deft, gentle fingers pressing down the keys.
Your heartstrings waltz along.
Your eyes, closed.
A melody beyond compare.
Inhale
Exhale
Voice.
The most beautiful sound.
Like the feeling of hot chocolate on a cold, snowy, Christmas Eve.
You're sitting near the fireplace.
Remember?
You were there.

Your voice hoarse,
You sang along.
With tears in your eyes and your heart in the heavens.
Smiling with the memory, your heart rises once more
to take its rightful place.
Swaying along to the sound.
Thrilled to your very core.
Roger's Place.
Bright lights.
The stage, just before your disbelieving eyes.
You're only nine rows away.
A childhood fantasy
finally come true.
Chords—
the end arrives.
You cheer, laugh, smile, and cry.
Never again will you experience a night so magical.
The music rings in your ears that night, the next day, and even now.
It was, and will forever be, the night of your life.
The record slows.
You lift the needle,
swimming in the memories of that whirlwind day.
You aren't religious, but you raise your heart to the heavens
and thank whatever may exist.
Thank you for the music.
Thank you for giving me Wings and teaching me to fly.

Untouched
A Poem by Cora Dallyn

An overwhelming wave of realization
I feel my throat constrict and adrenaline surge through me
My heart bursts and tears explode from my eyes.

A bed we have never shared
Untouched by your skin
No impressions
Or lived in history

A clean slate
Or a fresh start

I feel your fingers trace my spine
Your heart pressed against mine
My prescription to fall asleep
When our love was deep

Will I turn to look for you?
Does this bed prescribe dreams or nightmares?

Untitled
A Poem by Travis O'Neil

Where do I turn for help
When everyone expects
Something
When do I care for myself
If every moment idle is wasting

Responsibility,
Always got the best of me
The weight of all your
Expectations
And the ones I place on me

Am I the asshole, or do you see
Me trying
Will you count it as failure
If I quit before I'm dying,
If I told you I'm okay,
Believe me, I was lying

Through the Veil
A poem by Brandon Tilt

Look to the streets,
In between the walls of each skyscraper,
To see what's beyond the harbourside sunsets,
Crammed into alleyways to make room for the dog walkers,
Cloaked well by the sunflowers and yellow dogwoods,
Are the sunspots and weary eyes,
With cracked skin, and broken limbs.

You've never seen so many glittering clothing shops,
Where is the hospital, you might ask?
Most people probably couldn't even find it
as they peer through the bus window,
I hear the cries of agony muffled by traffic,
I see the tears which are lost as they pool
into puddles immersed with raindrops,
Where the icy sidewalks imprison each drop,
Like a time capsule, suspended,
Until the downpour washes it all away.

Yesterday I saw a grown man cry,
He begged me with a gentle whimper: "Please don't hurt me",
Traumatized, after thieves stole his prescription medication,
He told me…
That predators wait outside the hospital,
Patiently waiting for their chance to strike,
So as I approached him at the bus stop and talked with him,
He thought I might attack him too,
When I simply offered him a rolled joint,
A rare act of unconditional kindness,
At a time where I felt like he really needed it.
Steps away, I found an elderly indigenous man,
Next to him, his walker and some grocery bags,

We talked for a bit while waiting for the bus,
He was homeless, and had been for over 60 years,
And told me that he recently quit drinking,
I smiled as we spoke,
He was very friendly and I could tell he had a good heart.
But at that moment, some themes struck me and hit deep,
Colonialism, Capitalism, The Fentanyl Crisis,
We humans did this,
Created countless victims of horrendous injustice,
With each voice representing millions more.

Out in Squamish nation there are eldery protestors at the Wet'suwet'en pipeline,
Who face unspeakable violence and racism, defending what is rightfully theirs,
Why do we as a society fund the violent abuse of elderly indigenous people,
It would make more sense to respond
to the disastrous floods all over British Columbia,
The consequences of ecocide are scars,
Which do not fully heal, Like trauma, but to the planet itself,
But who really cares, We'd rather talk about Bitcoin, or Netflix
The almighty dollar, That which pollutes the mind, And rapes the earth.
Seriously, how much more consumption can we even handle?
Will we ever have enough?
What is happening?   O...Canada...
Why do we still prioritize corporate greed?   O...Canada...
Why do we displace and disempower
the stewards of the earth?   O...Canada...
Why can't we recognize that this earthly drama is our own sinking ship?
I see the pain of the streets embodying the corruption of the masses,
With each echo of suffering ringing out like a distress call from the planet itself,
When will we put the cycles of trauma and suffering to rest?

When will we begin to listen?

As above, so below;

As below, so above.

The Protagonist
A poem by Electus

I am the protagonist.
The world is sketched before my eyes and erased behind me.
My steps serve as this planet's melodious heartbeat.
The wind blows only to fill my lungs.
Thoughts fuel my existence, and sounds, which come as
whispers of guidance, direct my path.
I have been sculpted by his own hands; a master designer's masterpiece.
I am different; truly significant.
However, much to my dismay,
Everyone is a protagonist.

Life's Poem
A poem by Electus

Life is not a math problem that must be solved,
Rather it's a poem written in your own words.

Wildflower
A poem by Samantha Skeich

For so long, I believed I was broken,
Poisoned with "you're not enough"
"You're too hard to love"
I resented the cobwebs that took stake in my heart
And succumbed to the water that drowned my lungs.
I felt like a wasteland.
Then.
There was you.
You did not fix me. Because I am not broken.
You didn't hold me down,
Forcing me to drown.
You love my "too much" and you
Plant seeds when I don't feel I am enough.
You opened a window and allowed my heart to grow.
You gave me breath where lungs once threatened to overflow.
I'd breathe you in forever if it meant
Wildflowers in my heart
And sunlight in my lungs.

The Drive
A poem by Samantha Skeich

I'd drive through heat waves
And canola fields as yellow as the sunlight you show

I'd drive through thunderstorms
In the sky
And in my chest

I'd drive up ten mountains covered in snow
And through forests as green as your eyes

I used to hate driving;

But I'd drive to you forever.

Coping
A poem by Josh Harnack

My 9 to 5 is 24/7
Thirst only quenched by the manna of heaven.
With gold coloured pigment I hide my plight
I shall not go easy into that good night.

Drowning in content, treading for art.
Staying afloat, before I depart.
Restless at night, burned out by day.
Creativity, running astray.

Slapping down pigment what's to explain.
If I keep doubling down I'll go insane.
Chained to my mind, trapped in confusion.
I just tell myself it's all an illusion.

Addicted to the struggle
Intrusive thoughts clouding the mind
Fleeting freedom caught in the grind
The weight of life holding me down
Just two more weeks to earn my crown

I am almost there, the taste is sweet
So excited I am losing sleep.
But the tank is low, it's almost empty.
I can see the end so do not tempt me.

The clock ticks fast, I am running slow
Not enough time to put on this show.
Perfection's a curse, a waste of time.
The iron is hot, it's in its prime.
I'm in the way, and I cannot move
Fucking Go! I have something to prove.
I will not fail, I won't allow it.
The show will go on and that's a promise.

The Sabotage Loop
A poem by Kian Isaac

It starts with a plan. A plan to get your life together.
You tell yourself you're gonna eat healthier, exercise more, drink less.
Maybe, you'll buy yourself a planner and then
you say you're gonna be more productive.
You say, "I'll start being nicer to everyone and myself"
"I'll do more self care"
"I'll finally become one of those humans, the ones who are perfect with
 their life together, the part of their life you see on social media anyway.
The ones who wake up early and get everything done.
Except it's already 3am and this urge came from nowhere.
It's too late to do anything now, and when the sun finally rolls around,
you're too exhausted to remember what the full plan even was,
you tell yourself…
"I'll start tomorrow" and you reason with, it's better to start things
on a monday anyway. It eases the guilt a little bit.
Tomorrow never comes.
You tell yourself the same thing on Monday.
Every Monday.
Like a merry-go-round that never stops.
I call this…
"The Sabotage Loop"

For Nelson
A poem by Kristopher Hinz

The Rebellious Dignitary:
Set apart for a rural lifestyle in which your wisdom would be put to more traditional use as a chieftain, you ran away to the city, breaking barriers and boundaries as the first all-black law firm.

In this period, you inspired me to do more than is expected, even when they say you cannot. It is always impossible until it is done. You inspired me to hold fast to my path and have faith in my own power to shape my destiny.

The Determined Advocate:
Blazing a new trail, you resolved to defend the defenseless in the face of a cruel and cold legal system that denied you the right to use the same toilet, train or township as those of a lighter hue.

In this period, you inspire me to stand for what is right, even when that has left me standing alone.

The Flawed Hero:
The convicted terrorist. The lover of many women. The absent father who was too committed to a greater goal.

In this period, you hurt many and were hurt by many more. You taught me that a saint is simply a sinner that keeps on trying. A bump in the road should not be enough for me to call off the journey. I will keep going and seek forgiveness even when I slip and transgress. You remind me there is richness and growth to be found in every dark period and that a flower needs an equal measure of rain and sunshine to bloom.

The Dignified Prisoner:
For nearly 30 years, you are locked away in your fight for justice. It is to that small cell that I wish to one day make my greatest pilgrimage. Over the course of 9000 days, you better yourself with humility and strength, learning the language and lifestyle of your oppressor and learning to love and appreciate his culture.

In this period, I learned from you your phrase "know your enemy and learn his favourite sport."

You inspired me to study sports journalism and to become the cultural chameleon you were, finding the good in every creed and country and acting as a friend to all.

The Eloquent Statesman:
With a display of forgiveness rarely seen, you guide your nation along a bright new path, demonstrating with word and deed that everyone has a right to safety and security in your country, embracing even the widow whose husband invented Aparthied. You traverse the globe, speaking with a baritone so rich it makes even the greatest orators seem squeaky.

In this period, your carefully chosen words and forgiving acts inspire me to love, love and love again when I am hurt by those I treasure. When extended family have not accepted my colour, it is your example I turn to when I must find the strength to find conciliation and not confrontation.

The power of your eloquence inspires me to study public relations and to continue to express my pain, love and joy with the stroke of my pen.

My Hero:
In the face of unparalleled humanity and an unshakable dignity, love triumphs over hate. You are once again my guiding light as I seek a new career path.

I love you, Nelson.

Bitter
A Poem by Stefani Litwin

I told you I was tired of fighting for us and
That my cup was running empty.
You took your overflowing cup
And watered her garden.

Still Bitter
A Poem by Stefani Litwin

I wish I could hurt you
Make you feel the pain that I feel
Pain that you caused.
But I never could,
And that's the difference between you and me.

Jim Carrey
A Song by Brey

I don't actually like Walt Disney
Or Jim Carrey's, The Grinch
Just haven't been happy
20 years since

And it reminds me
Of simpler times
Now I see
Your fucking point

I live off nostalgia, shit
I wanna quit
Get over it
And really live
I wanna be passionate
Fully commit
And get a grip

Forget participation
And high school football games
Lighten up under the bleachers
Setting shit aflame

It reminds me
Of simpler times
Now I see
Your fucking point

I live on
Shitttt, Awooo
Shitttt, Awooo
But not today
I lose

I was drunk when I wrote this song
I lack the substance to carry it along
And I'm running on nostalgic fumes
I'd rather be chasing something brand new

And I'm running on nostalgic fumes
I'd rather be chasing something brand new

Shitttt, Awooo
Shitttt, Awooo
But not today
I lose…

The Unspoken Poet
A poem by Brandon Tilt

Among crumpled pieces of paper, and cigarette ashes,
There exists a burrowing inner sadness, just waiting to pour out,
But it's far easier to bite your tongue than to speak the truth,

Sunken into your seat at the weekly poetry slam,
You do your best to tune out the chatter from the booths nearby,
Your eyes brighten, and soften, in unison with each poet's performance,
Witnessing the transformative power of the stage,
Seeing what once was a tortured sadness slip away,
With each word reflecting this look in their eye,
Of empowerment and reclamation.

So you begin to tell yourself,
"I need to get up there.",
"I can only imagine just how good it feels to be that free.",

You hold back the tears you want to cry for this wild, untamed poet,
You're jealous, eager to let it all pour out,
But…for you…that's just too…abnormal,
So you hold back,
Those unrelenting tears,
Let them burrow into even darker holes,
Unexpressed, buried under a mound of doubt,

These are the caged feelings of the unspoken poet.
The key is where it's always been, where it forever remains
It quietly dangles, fastened around your neck,
And although you know it's closeby…you can't ever find it
You never could unlock the cage,
So you stopped writing love poems,
It's not…"normal" to show such deep appreciation and admiration,
In a world where kindness is a crux,

Where gentleness is a weakness,
And when society wants to knock you down
it goes straight for the heart,

They restrict you,
They monitor and filter your voice,
To keep you muzzled,
You might even tell yourself:

"Yeah, It's better to stay quiet",

"It's the norm",

"It's safer this way",

"To stay where nobody can hurt you",

You may have even fooled yourself,
Into believing that it's better to forever remain,
the unspoken—
Poet.

Rotten too
A Poem by Sabryn Jones

Sorry about throwing up in the back of the cab — I wasn't drunk

unfortunately I'm just like that, I'm just living life with a tight stomach waiting for something to break

I should probably get drunk and maybe people would like me more

my family joked once that I would have an ulcer before I was 25

3 years to go so give me something to worry about

I watch the apples I bought sit on the counter and nobody reaches for them — they begin to bruise, they begin to rot, I don't throw them out

red and round turned to brown sludge in the fruit bowl

still no one's throws them out

the flies will come soon, the way they always do when things die and decay, I'll sit in the kitchen and watch the black masses buzz around me until there's nothing left to worry about

Folktales for the Dead
A Poem by Sabryn Jones

you believe in folktales like a little kid because girls
can sleep in beds with girls and nobody dies

well maybe people die but it's not bloody lips,
shattered ribs, rope burn wrists and that's enough for you

because you'll probably die—you're ten years old
and you know that girls who dreams about red lips
and softer skin are meant to die

folktales have the big bad wolf and the green skinned witches a
nd you try to believe that you're not like them

you're not the one eating children—you don't lie about your intentions

you know you should—nobody likes it when girls stand
too close to their friends and trade lip gloss in the back room

you should lie and say tommy felt under your skirt and you didn't go
home and burn your thigh to try and get rid of what he left behind

if you tell people anyone that sarah touched your hand then
the town will chase you out with pitchforks and burning books

it doesn't matter that you didn't eat children—that you didn't poison the well

you did something far worse

you believed in a happy ending

Post-Anxiety
A poem by Electus

The clouds are shaking,
The breeze is overwhelming,
The fear of what is to come is ever growing.
Time rolls with the wind,
And ever so gently,
Rain arrives.

Tomorrow
A Poem by Electus

The sun will rise again tomorrow,
the birds will sing their songs.
The wind will whistle of love and sorrow,
the trees will wave their palms.

The flowers will bloom again tomorrow,
there may be some rain.
The lightning will strike like bow and arrow,
the twilight sky will be a painting.

The grass tomorrow will surely be greener,
enough to awaken the eyes of this dreamer.

Tomorrow is near alas; Soon this night too shall pass.

Bromeliad
A Poem by Ashley Witiw

Bromeliad of shining bodice and bright golden crown,
Resting centerfold in the windowsill of a botanist self-styled,
Bathing her in the gossamer sunshine of his admiration,
Proclaiming she is the one his heart is most fond of
To all other flowers in his garden.

Bromeliad of shining bodice and golden crown,
Resting centerfold in the windowsill of a botanist self-styled,
Her vibrant colour transitions as her mother and those before,
Feeding her with the honeyed words of affection
He loves her, says he, for who she becomes.

Bromeliad of shining bodice and greening crown,
Resting centerfold in the windowsill of a botanist self-styled,
Searching for that which he swears is growth he catered,
He tires of shining green and searches for colour,
Finding imperfections, he disdains her.

Bromeliad of dulling bodice and crown removed,
Lying in the refuse wastes of a botanist self-styled,
In the centerfold of the windowsill rests another,
Bathing in the gossamer sunshine of his affection,
Bromeliad of shining bodice and bright violet crow.

Hollow
A poem by Ashley Witiw

As brittle branches of endless winter
I am hollow, broken and despair
My soul is tangled in darkest night
Dawn signals no return.

Slipping
A poem by Samantha Skeich

For so long, two hands have held me
And told me,
"It's going to be alright"
For so long, those hands held me,
And I,
held theirs too.

Everytime I fall
And scrape my knees,
Those two hands have caught me'
"I'll give you a band-aid;
Take it, please".

Unfamiliar hands, not quite like theirs,
Reached out,
Offering me a rebound.
Shushing my mouth,
"Our secret", they said.
"Is safe and sound".

And now those hands have come back,
Tight hold and gripping at my throat,
You've made me feel shameful.

I'm longing for hands that once kept me afloat.

Now my hands are not mine,
They're shaky and unsure
Maybe it's a sign
To protect theirs from more hurt.
My knees are left scraped,
In an attempt to be alone.
But I can't stand stained hands
So I only rely on my own.

Enthralled
A poem by Rebecca Ryan

The darkness inside me has a mind of its own,
And it took me a long time until I realised that her
Thoughts were never my own.

Oh she was convincing,
The darkness,
Never ending,
She sowed within me
Seeds of insanity,
Sprouting toxins,
Blooming malice.

Her endlessly persistent,
Persuasive ideas had slithered their way into the recesses of my mind..

Her forked tongue,
Whispered perversions,
Gaslighting me into submission,
Kneeling before her falseness,
Revelling in the uncertainty,
The naivety,
The brutality of her love.

My sanctuary,
Lay sullied,
Made into her throne,

I,
made into a fool.

Love, I Loved You
A poem by Madeline Medensky

he slips into me hard, my

pantyhose runs in wire-like cuts

the brown hair slicked, short sides, clean front

blue eyes spherical or centering or clear

I burst with my femininity, all over

with red blood lines and thick black jelly-like things things

opening up inside of me (an egg crushing, picked away)

and I want him to say "beautiful" or "gorgeous" or "that's ok"

but isn't it great he doesn't, cause I loved him he says

(instead) "shit…really?" and his eyes pout down, sinking,

closed down - "at least suck me out?"

I wouldn't I won't

I didn't I don't.

Giants, I'm Just a Girl
A poem by Madeline Medensky

I stand in a room of giants
hardly standing
sitting with paperweight faces
marked by their non-polarity
a proud forehead, eyes like stones
I stand in a room of giants
in their English-own
needle arms, thick collarbones, a sterile chin
my own could never torment so
I stand in a room of giants
and listen in
giants to giantness believe
the world made for them
doorways sometimes are too little and too thin
I manage through
they speak too
unwrinkling a thought
I forgot the world occurs in standing
between the knowing what you're not
and then the needing of its proof.

Inferno
A Poem by Peter Anto Johnson

Why do I ignite trembling disgust?
Grotesque disgust sparked trigger
Not without quivering shivers dust
A day's rampage won't bring relief
All that is shallow is not anguish,
Only sinking, by all account so deep
An anguish that does not extinguish
Abysmal slumbers let it seep
The hate that's really stalling
Above all others is the passion
Floating loathing and writhing
When can I end this emotion?

Morning rage
A Poem by John Christy Johnson

Whose temper is that? That furrows his brow.
Its owner turns tantrums into objects to throw
Like a burning bush, his fury burns a bright red glow
I watch him pace. To and fro...
He gives his fists a shake,
And screams I've made a bad mistake.
The echoes of his holler break,
The fragile silence that makes the sleeping wake.
The anger is blood-fueled, fiery, and deep,
But he has responsibilities to keep,
Tormented with nightmares he never sleeps.
Tossing and turning anguished, he never weeps.
He rises from his cursed bed,
With thoughts of violence in his head,
A flash of rage and he sees red.
Without a pause I turned and fled.

I'm the girl
A poem by Stefani Litwin

I'm scared I will never truly be loved the way I love.
I feel like a placeholder.
I'm the girl who will listen to your trauma
And put you back together when you're falling apart
I'm the girl who loves with her whole heart despite it being ripped out
so many times in the past.
I'm the girl who teaches you how to love the next girl better
I'm the girl who will love you unconditionally
Why is it so impossible to get that back?

I don't wanna love you anymore
A poem by Stefani Litwin

I don't wanna love you anymore
I don't wanna think about you every day
Wonder what you're doing or who you're with
I wish you would've cut the bullshit and ended the lies
I wish we cut our love story short
I don't wanna love you anymore
When you're out loving someone else
the way you should've loved me.

Ever Since
A poem by Daniel Klassen

Greater than
Loyalty, honour, and respect
Greater than
Best friends, real good-byes, and regrets
That night, in your backyard, sitting by the fire
You said we were brothers
Today I may safely assume
That family means nothing to you
Shifting allegiance to where your addiction
It is encouraged, even celebrated
So this is how it feels
Spending ten years
Of your life
Chasing nothing
All of that energy
Purchasing nothing
But a regrettable
Experience
Ever since
You lied
The sunburst
Orange flames
Oh, but I must thank you for
Spilling fire on my gasoline
I am inspired by the malice you
Have placed inside of me
Keep on lying to yourself
I sleep soundly despite
That grinding noise my
Fractured bones make

Head Tilt Chin Lift
A poem by Daniel Klassen

Yeah, kid, I know
Life is hard sometimes
I know girls will
Break your heart
You were born
With an ugly face
Into an average
Low-income family
Just ask your mother
About your brother
Who was aborted
She could not take the pain
Of raising a child
In this forsaken place
You need to deal with it
Reality is a hypocrite
Life is about lifting iron
To save yourself
From the hell that is
Surrounding us
Mitigating only so much stress
With the bench press
Wanting more than what
The weights can give us
It's about true friends
The people who will
Forfeit anything
For you, in the end
Looking in the mirror
Asking one question
Today, did I do the best
To make an example of myself

Sirens
A song by Brandon Tilt

Do you hear the sirens,
Do you hear the silence,
Si-rens, flashing red with a full moon overhead,
The howls and cries of the sufferin,
Wheels turnin',
Rubber burnin',
Soles worn in, head be spinnin' from da' sick-ness
Da' quietness... is
A song of vio-lence.

Soiled streets, filled with emp-ty smiles,
Damp alleys littered with pipes n' vials
Always breathing in the smell of burning plastic,
Halting traffic, and gazing outward with a blank stare,
Tirelessly bearing the cold night air,
Swore to your mother, this would be your last hit
Don' ask because they know you don' care.

One cold wet night on a Saturday,
The sun was setting on Mainstreet,
Many hungry spirits were out and walkin'
Your legs bleed, but there is no stoppin',
You cannot catch your breath... for fear of death,
The heart's a lab-yr-inth, of pain and confusion,
Searching desperately for one more hit of meth,
Your mind, a symphony of vio-lent music

Contusions, stop you dead in your tracks
Just another reason for you to stop usin',
But like clockwork, another withdrawal attacks,
Your tears blur your eyes and form an illusion,
You see a childhood friend with his arms outstretched,

You go to hug them, but it's a needle instead,
The blaring of the ambulance brings you to your senses,
Driven senseless,
While seeking solace

Do you hear the sirens,
Can you hear the silence,
Vio-lence,
Heroes breathin' life into victims of the poison,
Joy's end—
Da' quietness... is

A song of vio-lence
*Drumming stops
Do you hear the sirens,
Can you hear the silence, (more quietly)
Can you hear the silence, (more quietly)
A song of viol-lence (whisper)

Untitled
A poem by Mark O'Reilly

A night passes enjoyed but unrecorded
as a half-sung dirge of nonsense
lulls me to not-quite-sleep.

So is that how it was meant to go?
It's best to leave such questions in your throat.
Or better yet, settle them back down with another slug.

Half-hearted belts of song punctuate the evening,
The rye sees more sincerity but offers none in return.
Gone but not forgotten, or so we'd like to think.

The familiar scent of an adored enemy can hardly be avoided
as the drips and drabs of strangers' adventures seep out into the air.
All we can do is breathe deep, buckle up and stroll on,
secure as well as soaked to the bone by the admission that this is forever.

Untitled
A poem by JJ

Some never understand you,
Nor never even try to,
No matter what you do,
Or how you try to improve.

Live your life without them,
Prove 'em wrong, ahem.
Grow; no need to condemn,
They're the ones hemmed.

Remember moments you've been
Betrayed.
Do better everyday.

I don't know how long it's been
A poem by Rebecca Ryan

You wouldn't recognize me,
if I passed you on the streets.
You don't know me anymore,
and I find solace in the fact.

The final goodbye.

Unknown
A poem by Isabella Anderson

As the wind blows,
My heart lows,
I feel this when life calls,
Everytime my heart falls,
A load of sadness,
That creates madness,
Feelings of being alone,
Brings the shivers of the unknown.

Peter Paranoia
A poem by Daniel Klassen

You had my back - When they stood still
You had my back - When no one gave a care
You had my back - Kill or be killed
You had my back - Turning mine on yours
Restless walks
Through suburban parks
Not knowing what to do
With all these calories
Keep it punk rock
Let mall security know
what you're all about
Skateboards breaking windows
So many leaders
And inspiring writers
Have fallen and
Are now breaking down
Drinking whiskey in back alleys during winter storms
The static I hear every day is
A reminder of the good times
And how quickly they can die
You were too good for Earth
The pain and the remedy, to remind us of you
Empty feelings in my guts are depleting
What's left of the timid strength fading inside of me
When you replace love with something that holds you back
Take a deep breath
Peter, tell me about the time you carved
A path into life, teaching us how to smoke the cherry out
I took your life for granted
I did not cherish the fleeting seconds that we shared
Appreciating these moments with your ghost
Seeking confidence in your rest

Overdraft
A poem by Daniel Klassen

Having the world on my shoulders
All of this negativity and recession
Living in these hard times
I am a challenger; put me to the test
Sometimes I wake up
Wishing I could sleep forever
Reassuring myself
Not to go mad
I've been through anguish
Humility and petty crimes
Things are getting worse
So I'm going back to my old ways
Would you call me a sell-out?
If I left the hood?
Or would you wish me good luck,
As I drove away?
I think I've seen
More than I can take
But last impressions are
Often getting me down
I have seen the colour
of your bloodshot eyes
I've heard the lies that
you preach to yourself
Are you proud of
The work you have done?
Standing on top
Of shaky ground
Nothing but a short buzz
There is no tolerance
We dig drugs out of the
The ground in this province

Edgelord
A Poem by Brey

I'm not laughing cause you're funny

I'm laughing because I am uncomfortable

You think you're so edgy

But I think you are stupid

Not stupid, like stupid

But stupid, like stupid

My mom taught me to let it go

But I honestly can't

Cause my stomach hurts when you're around

I hate your 'opinion'

Cause it's harmful to others

I hate your 'opinion'

Because it makes you stronger

So shut up and talk to someone else

Cause I'd rather be alone

Than be with your stupidity

Untitled
A Poem by Tianna

You don't like cherry
But that's how I taste
Why lick a lolly
That just goes to waste
Don't open the wrapper
If you're just gonna chuck it
If you want someone else
Then you can go suck it.

Cavalier
A Poem by Riley Witiw

You are cavalier, but never clear,
stirring ripples in mirages
But not a drop of truth is here,
and the flowing water pauses
Revealing deserts and desolation
where vultures dine on the asphalt
Well lick your lips, bird of predation
I am your parched prey.

Loosen my binds, I fall from the mast
her voice, guileful and sweet
But still, I fall into siren's grasp
and she drags me by my feet.
Descending into a midst of blue
full of water unfit to quench
I will spit the salt in my own wounds
and restore myself as I lose my breath.

We are more than justified
in our actions, arise
and stand against the tyrants
Who hold our heads
beneath the surface line.
They're content if we die.
They'll rule without us in their lives.

Synopsis

What better way to scream at, or about, the world than through poetry?
This book is sewn together by creatives who are hurting and healing,
thriving or just surviving,
getting up everyday and putting themselves out there.
For what?
To connect with you. To see you.
That's right. We see you.
We see your pain, your love, your fears, your joy.
Come, relate with us about the trials and tribulations
of living in this crazy world.

www.ingramcontent.com/pod-product-compliance
Lightning Source LLC
Chambersburg PA
CBHW030506220526
45464CB00006B/2675